THE SIERRA CLU
HOME PLANET POSTCARD C

D0526895

IMAGES FROM
THE HOME PLANET

BY KEVIN W. KELLEY
FOR THE ASSOCIATION
OF SPACE EXPLORERS

Sierra Club Books

"The first day or so we all pointed to our countries. The third or fourth day we were pointing to our continents. By the fifth day we were aware of only one Earth."

Sultan Bin Salman al-Saud
Saudi Arabia

The Sierra Club, founded in 1892 by John Muir, has devoted itself to the study and protection of the Earth's scenic and ecological resources—mountains, wetlands, woodlands, wild shores and rivers, deserts and plains. The publishing program of the Sierra Club offers books to the public as a nonprofit educational service in the hope that they may enlarge the public's understanding of the Club's basic concerns. The point of view expressed in each book, however, does not necessarily represent that of the Club. The Sierra Club has some sixty chapters coast to coast, in Canada, Hawaii, and Alaska. For information about how you may participate in its programs to preserve wilderness and the quality of life, please address inquiries to Sierra Club, 730 Polk Street, San Francisco, CA 94109.

A note to the respondent: these slightly oversized postcards require the same postage as a first-class letter.

This collection is based on the book *The Home Planet,* which was published in 1988 by Addison-Wesley, Inc.

Cover: Africa and the Indian Ocean.
Title page: Earth from 10,000 miles.

Production by Felicity Gorden and Bonnie Smetts
Book design and cover design by Bonnie Smetts
Composition by Classic Typography, Ukiah, CA
Printed by South Sea International Press Ltd., Hong Kong

10 9 8 7 6 5 4 3 2 1

Introduction

On December 7, 1972, in the infinite blackness of space, 21,750 nautical miles from Earth, an astronaut speeding at nearly seven miles a second toward the moon held up his camera and pointed it toward home. Then, for one brief fraction of a second, he released the shutter and allowed billions of photons of light born on the sun eight minutes earlier, which reflected off nearly half the surface of the planet, to rush through his lens, to activate a thin layer of light-sensitive photo emulsion, and to form the first picture showing the full Earth.

Thus we began to realize astronomer Frederick Hoyle's great prophecy that "Once a photograph of the Earth taken from the outside is available, a new idea as powerful as any in history will be let loose."

Some two decades after this famous first image of the whole Earth was taken, we are beginning to grasp that idea: that all life forms are interconnected and interdependent and that they are all part of one great living membrane that encompasses our entire planet: Mother Earth.

Some aboriginal and ancient peoples knew this to be true instinctively. For us, however, the images of the Earth from space can awaken that realization. The pictures elicit a sense of awe and wonder, and serve to remind us of the great mystery of existence, what Joseph Campbell called the "ultimate religious experience."

The view of Earth is indeed a glimpse of divinity. Photographs of our home from space are the icons of that epiphany. With our perception of them comes a sense of reverence and, I believe, it is this reverence that will save us; it will turn our world around.

Kevin W. Kelley
Bolinas, California

KEVIN W. KELLEY is an artist and photographer who lives in Bolinas, California. His underlying interest is in the integration of art, science and spirit with special emphasis on using visual imagery to illuminate perception. He envisioned *The Home Planet* as a tool to rekindle a sense of mystery, awe, and grace in our world.

"Suddenly from behind the rim of the moon, in long, slow-motion moments of immense majesty, there emerges a sparkling blue and white jewel, a light, delicate sky-blue sphere laced with slowly swirling veils of white, rising gradually like a small pearl in a thick sea of black mystery.

"It takes more than a moment to fully realize this is Earth . . . home."

Edgar Mitchell
USA

Earthrise as seen from the moon.

From *The Sierra Club Home Planet Postcard Collection*, by Kevin W. Kelley, for the Association of Space Explorers.

"Space is so close: It took only eight minutes to get there and twenty to get back."
                                            Wubbo Ockels
                                            Netherlands

Cosmonauts at the Kosmodrome Baikonur.

From *The Sierra Club Home Planet Postcard Collection*, by Kevin W. Kelley, for the Association of Space Explorers.

"You see 16 sunrises every day you're in space. No sunrise is ever the same. . . . The sun truly 'comes up like thunder,' and it sets just as fast. . . . But in that time you see at least eight different bands of color come and go, from a brilliant red to the brightest and deepest blue."

Joseph Allen
USA

Sunset lit by Earth's atmosphere.

From *The Sierra Club Home Planet Postcard Collection,* by Kevin W. Kelley, for the Association of Space Explorers. Text copyright 1983 by Joseph Allen and reprinted with the permission of Omni Publications International Limited.

"The Earth was small, light blue, and so touchingly alone, our home that must be defended like a holy relic." Aleksei Leonov
USSR

Mozambique Channel, Madagascar.

From *The Sierra Club Home Planet Postcard Collection,* by Kevin W. Kelley, for the Association of Space Explorers. Text used by permission of Michael Woods, Senior Editor, the *Toledo Blade.*

"Before I flew I was already aware of how small and vulnerable our planet is; but only when I saw it from space, in all its ineffable beauty and fragility, did I realize that humankind's most urgent task is to cherish and preserve it for future generations."

Sigmund Jahn
German Democratic Republic

The Atlantic coast of South Africa.

From *The Sierra Club Home Planet Postcard Collection,* by Kevin W. Kelley, for the Association of Space Explorers.

"On the return trip home, gazing through 240,000 miles of space toward the stars and the planet from which I had come, I suddenly experienced the universe as intelligent, loving, harmonious."

Edgar Mitchell
USA

Africa, Europe and western USSR.

From *The Sierra Club Home Planet Postcard Collection,* by Kevin W. Kelley, for the Association of Space Explorers.

"This beauty consists of subtle nuances, as in the miraculous balance of soft and brilliant hues. Only a child in its innocence could apprehend the purity and splendor of this vision."

Patrick Baudry
France

Linear dunes, Namibian Desert.

From *The Sierra Club Home Planet Postcard Collection,* by Kevin W. Kelley, for the Association of Space Explorers.

"I used to have dreams when I was a kid that I'd go running down the street and jump up in the air and go flying and just fly through the air all by myself. That's what weightlessness is like."

Robert Gibson
USA

The first unattached space walk.

From *The Sierra Club Home Planet Postcard Collection*, by Kevin W. Kelley, for the Association of Space Explorers. Text used courtesy of "Frontline."

"When the Russian cosmonaut tells me that the atmosphere over Lake Baikal is as polluted as it is over Europe, and when the American astronaut tells me that fifteen years ago he could take much clearer pictures of the industrial centers than today, then I am getting concerned."　　Ernst Messerschmid
　　　　　　　　　　　　　　Federal Republic of Germany

The Indian Ocean near Madagascar.

From *The Sierra Club Home Planet Postcard Collection,* by Kevin W. Kelley, for the Association of Space Explorers.

"After several weeks it became difficult to remember clearly the fragrance of grass and trees, or warm summer rain, or powdery snow in a glade, or the faces of friends and loved ones that you now see only in dreams."

Pyotr Klimuk
USSR

Snow cover in Desolation Canyon, Utah, USA.

From *The Sierra Club Home Planet Postcard Collection,* by Kevin W. Kelley, for the Association of Space Explorers.

"When you look out the other way toward the stars you realize it's an awful long way to the next watering hole." Loren Acton
USA

Laguna Verde in the Andes Mountains.

From *The Sierra Club Home Planet Postcard Collection,* by Kevin W. Kelley, for the Association of Space Explorers.

Now I know why I'm here.
Not for a closer look at the moon,
But to look back
At our home
The Earth.

Alfred Worden
USA

The Earth rising over the moon.

From *The Sierra Club Home Planet Postcard Collection,* by Kevin W. Kelley, for the Association of Space Explorers.

"The tremendous brightness of light in space came as a surprise to me. . . . It was so dazzling I forgot I was looking through a dense filter. When I lifted the filter (strictly speaking, this is not allowed, but the temptation was too great) the sun shone so brightly on my right that it was impossible to look in that direction."

Yevgeni Khrunov
USSR

Cosmonaut working in open space.

From *The Sierra Club Home Planet Postcard Collection*, by Kevin W. Kelley, for the Association of Space Explorers.

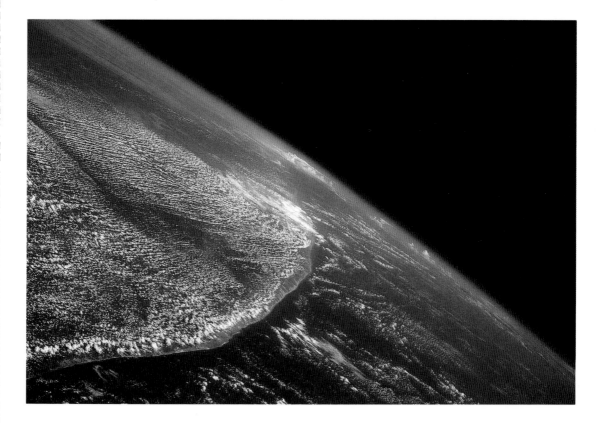

"For the first time in my life I saw the horizon as a curved line. It was accentuated by a thin seam of dark blue light — our atmosphere. Obviously this was not the ocean of air I had been told it was so many times in my life. I was terrified by its fragile appearance."

Ulf Merbold
Federal Republic of Germany

Eastern coast of Somalia.

From *The Sierra Club Home Planet Postcard Collection,* by Kevin W. Kelley, for the Association of Space Explorers.

"It isn't important in which sea or lake you observe a slick of pollution, or in the forests of which country a fire breaks out, or on which continent a hurricane arises. You are standing guard over the whole of our Earth."

Yuri Artyukhin
USSR

Tropical storm "Xina" over the Pacific.

From *The Sierra Club Home Planet Postcard Collection,* by Kevin W. Kelley, for the Association of Space Explorers.

"While out there in orbit, dreams were usually about Earth."
Vladimir Lyakhov
USSR

Bahama Islands.

From *The Sierra Club Home Planet Postcard Collection,* by Kevin W. Kelley, for the Association of Space Explorers. Text from James E. Oberg and Alcestis R. Oberg, *Pioneering Space,* New York: McGraw-Hill, 1968.

"Lebedev had never before grown plants, but on the station he used to rush off to our 'Oazis' installation every morning almost before his eyes were opened. He was growing peas and oats there."

Anatoli Berezovoy
USSR

Coastal tidelands, Bay of Bengal, Burma.

From *The Sierra Club Home Planet Postcard Collection,* by Kevin W. Kelley, for the Association of Space Explorers.

"We spent most of the way home discussing what color the moon was."

Eugene Cernan
USA

The lunar surface.

From *The Sierra Club Home Planet Postcard Collection*, by Kevin W. Kelley, for the Association of Space Explorers.

"The peaks were the recognition that it is a harmonious, purposeful, creating universe. The valleys came in recognizing that humanity wasn't behaving in accordance with that knowledge."

Edgar Mitchell
USA

The Greater Himalayas.

From *The Sierra Club Home Planet Postcard Collection,* by Kevin W. Kelley, for the Association of Space Explorers.

"My view of our planet was a glimpse of divinity." Edgar Mitchell
USA

Dawn over the Atlantic Ocean.

From *The Sierra Club Home Planet Postcard Collection,* by Kevin W. Kelley, for the Association of Space Explorers.

"Weightlessness comes on abruptly. I soared as if I was inside a soap bubble. Like an infant in the womb of my spacecraft, still a child of my Mother Earth." Miroslav Hermaszewski
Poland

The spacecraft *Challenger*.

From *The Sierra Club Home Planet Postcard Collection,* by Kevin W. Kelley, for the Association of Space Explorers.

"We went to the moon as technicians; we returned as humanitarians."   Edgar Mitchell
USA

The Earth rising above the moon.

From *The Sierra Club Home Planet Postcard Collection,* by Kevin W. Kelley, for the Association of Space Explorers.